Profile Your Target Market:

Build and use an avatar of your ideal customer or client

By

Scott A. Gardner

Copyright 2017 - Scott A. Gardner and
Agile' Marketing Services, LLC.

Other books by Scott A. Gardner:
Recognized Expert Status
Membership Site Design
Profitable Web Hosting

The author may have an affiliate relationship with some of the links listed in this book. He may receive a payment if you make a purchase.

Published by:
Dark Raptor Press
2nd Floor - Suite C
535 County Rt 54
Pennellville NY   13132
www.DarkRaptor.com
sales@DarkRaptor.com

Visit the authors website:
www.ScottGardnerAuthor.com

No part of this publication may be reproduced or disseminated in any form without the express written consent of the publisher, except in cases of short excerpts for the purpose of review.

First version (print & ebook) June 2017

All rights reserved.

Contents

What Is a Target Market?..1
What Is an Avatar?...6
Why Bother?..8
Demographics..10
Psychographics..13
Media and Entertainment..16
Food..19
Family...21
Work..23
Why Do You Buy?...25
Building the Avatar...28
Painting the Picture..31
Using Your Target Market Avatar..36
Who Is Like Your Avatar?..39
Where Do You Find Them?...42
What Are Their Pressure Points?...45
What Internal Conversation Can You Join?.............................49
Talk to the Individual...52
Connecting Via Social Media..56
Make a Connection...59
Help First...61
Build Your Avatar into Your Marketing Plan...........................64
Shared Stories...70
Acknowledgements..81

Scott A. Gardner

You hold in your hands an introduction to a powerful marketing principle. Getting to know your target market group allows you to anticipate their desires. It can seem as if you are actually reading their minds. Once you know them as a group, you can begin to create a profile of your ideal customer or prospect.

Who is your ideal customer? In a fantasy world, we'd all like customers who show up every day, place large high-profit orders, and pay cash on the spot. But in the real world, perhaps you're looking for customers who make more frequent purchases. Maybe you'd like to sell more high-profit products or services. Maybe you'd just like to find customers who pay quickly. You must develop a detailed description - a word picture, if you will - of your ideal customer or prospect.

After you've created a picture of the individual who is your ideal client, you can begin to use this avatar as a template for the real people you want as customers. This avatar will tell you where to find them, what they're interested in, and even what marketing messages will resonate with your prospects.

The whole process is shaped like an hourglass. You distill a large amount of information down to a small set of similar points. This is the description and personality of your ideal customer. Then, you'll

Profile Your Target Market

through the larger population to find people who are interested in your products or services.

I hope you find this book useful. If you apply the process to develop your target market avatar, and then use it to find prospects, I think you'll be very happy with the results.

I wish you health, happiness and prosperity!

Very best,

Scott A. Gardner

Congratulations on grabbing a copy of my book, *Profile Your Target Market!* If you apply the process inside, you'll see that it's easier than ever to find and communicate with prospects that could become clones of your ideal customer.

As a way of saying thanks, I'd like to give you a free book. Follow the link below to download a copy of my book, *Recognized Expert Status* (or choose another title - your choice).
 Just visit -

recex.ScottGardnerAuthor.com

Again, you have my sincere thanks. See you inside!

What Is a Target Market?

Many people starting a business, when asked about who is going to buy their products or services, say something like:

"Well, *people* are going to buy my stuff."

It's not just people beginning a business either. Some business people get lucky and start making sales, without actually trying to get a specific type of customer to buy from them.

In his book *Contemporary Marketing*, Dave Kurtz says that a target market is "a group of customers a business has decided to aim its marketing efforts and ultimately its merchandise towards." While it's not a bad definition, it's not really an explanation.

A better explanation, I think, is this: a target market is a group of people who share similar needs and wants that would be satisfied by purchasing your products or services. As a very broad example, if I were selling any type of automobile, I would be much better off focusing my attention on people who needed an automobile (either they don't have one, or the one they have needs to be replaced), rather than on "anyone who has a driver's license."

To refine things a bit, let's suppose I sell an expensive 2-seat sports cars, the Zeta Zipper, as my only product. Let's talk about who is NOT part of my target market: people who want a truck, families who have children, people who can't afford a sports car, people who are driven around by other people every day, and so forth. So of all the people who need or want a new automobile, only a small section of that larger group are even interested in buying the sports cars that I sell.

I can eliminate people who don't want, or can't afford, our sports cars from my marketing efforts. Rather than trying to hit "anyone with a license," I can concentrate my efforts on being seen by only the people who want and can afford my car. This allows me to focus our attention and marketing efforts. Laser focus.

The term "laser" originated as an acronym for "**light amplification by stimulated emission of radiation.**". Succinctly, a laser beam is a tightly (or highly) focused "bunch" of light (photons). Because it's tightly focused, it can stay bundled together for extremely long distances. We know how far away the moon is, for instance, because we can bounce a laser beam off its surface and measure the time it takes to get back to us. Lasers can also be made of just one color of light. (All colors together make "white" light.) So substances that only react to certain colors of light (red, as an example) might react to one laser, and not any other.

The fact that some things only react to certain colors of lasers is important. This concept extends to marketing and the messages we send out. The "color" of our particular message, say the fact that our sports car can go almost 500 miles on a tank of gas, will only resonate with people who are 1) in the market for a sports car, 2) can afford our sports car, and 3) want a car they don't have to fill up very often. I haven't said *why* it can go 500 miles on a tank. Perhaps it has an extremely large tank, or perhaps it gets superior gas mileage. Getting even more focused in our message - telling people exactly why it can go so far - will also narrow the group who is interested in our message.

I've been talking about the marketing messages we send out. What about our original question - what is a target audience? The two are joined at the root.

The focus of the marketing messages that you send out can define the target. That's putting the cart before the horse. But when you define the people you want to reach, you can then customize the messages that have the best chance of getting through to them despite all the "noise" in which we're each immersed on a daily basis.

This book is all about defining your target market and then being able to craft a message that cuts through the daily clutter to reach them. I tell my direct customers that you want to put yourself where prospects will trip over your message and you. I say this because most people who want or need your products and services will not be looking for you. How can they? They don't know you exist!

I recently spent quite a bit of time in San Francisco's Chinatown. The main street there is Grant. Most tourists don't really wander off Grant - perhaps 20%. And of all tourists, most don't go up Grant more than about 6 blocks. On the corner of the 5th block (Washington), there was a woman standing passing out colorful menus from a restaurant down the side of Washington. Her target market could be loosely defined as: hungry tourists at the corner of Grant and Washington who wanted to see food and prices from a Chinese restaurant. She was there from 11 AM to at least 10 PM every time I walked up Grant Ave, always trying to hand me a menu.

It's basic, but this is one way of defining your target market and trying to interact with them. Not everyone took a menu, but I saw people who did. Sometimes it was reflexive - that is, they took it because it was thrust at them. But other people actually looked at the menu. Of those that looked, some turned right and visited the restaurant. She was literally delivering her message by putting herself where her target audience would unknowingly find her. These were people who, a few moments before, didn't know that particular restaurant existed. By being there with a menu, she got customers for the restaurant.

The more you know about your target market (or target audience), the more tightly you can focus your messages (Yes, messages. Plural.) so you can be tripped over, or found, by those people.

Given all this, let's describe a target market this way: *A Target Market or Audience is a very narrow group of people that want or need your products/services. Because you understand them, you can enter the conversation already going on in their heads and introduce them to your products/services through laser focused messages in such a way as to get them to self-select as your customer or not.*

I'll be explaining the other points in my description that I haven't touched on here. I wanted you to understand that defining your target market, and customizing your messages so that they're seen and registered by those people, is essential to business success.

What Is an Avatar?

Once you know everything there is to know about the individuals who make up your target audience, you'll take all the points that make them similar to each other and write up a detailed description of that idealized person. You'll be able to describe not only where this person lives and their age, gender, and race but also what they do for entertainment and what they want out of life. You'll give them a name and know what they're thinking about: what keeps them up at night, and what makes them get out of bed in the morning. You will have an avatar for your target market.

An avatar is a description of your idealized customer. It's a detailed description of who this person is, where you find them, and the things they like and dislike. You'll describe what they do for recreation and how they trip over your messages.

Here's an important point: this is NOT a description just pulled out of the air. This is built by putting time, effort, and probably cash into research. If you're just starting your business or adding a totally new product or service, you'll have to go out and find these people. If you already have a business and want to define your ideal customer, you can start by interviewing your "best" current customers. It's also not a bad idea to interview your "worst" customers as well. Too much information, in this case, is a good start. The description you write should be based on the information of real people.

Once you write out the avatar's detailed description, you can begin writing marketing messages that directly address their concerns. You can then put them in places where your prospects will trip over them.

Why Bother?

What good is it defining your target market and writing up an avatar's detailed description? What can it actually do for you?

The first thing it will do for you is *save* you money. When you aren't trying to spread a generic message far and wide to the largest possible audience, your marketing costs will go down. You can send the same message to the same audience multiple times, increasing the chances that the audience will listen to it, rather than send a message once to a much larger audience.

The second thing that will happen is that you'll *make* money. If you're only hitting those folks who are predisposed to needing or wanting your products/services, they'll buy in higher percentages. If 2 people out of a hundred buy, that's 2%. But if 2 people out of 10 buy, that's 20%. You have a better chance by concentrating on the people making up the second group.

The best reason to focus on a target market is that you can make a larger profit. People who need or want your product/service are less interested in a low price than they are in something that meets their needs. You can raise your prices and also raise the quality and/or efficacy of what you're selling. I always tell my direct clients to raise their prices high enough to provide the best quality product or service that their market will buy. Once they raise their prices high enough that their current target market thinks it's too expensive, they need to find a new target market that doesn't (or come up with two different products and go after two target markets).

Refining the knowledge you have of your target market is like sharpening a knife. A dull knife will cut if you apply enough force, but a sharp knife leaves a clean cut with minimal effort. And it will cut exactly where you want it to. Remember our laser? A laser will cut even more precisely with even less effort! A knife is good, but a laser is better.

By defining your target market, you can target the exact people who want and can afford to buy what you're selling, while ignoring everyone else who has no interest in your products/services. It allows you to concentrate your time, effort, and money where it will be most productive for you.

Demographics

When you begin researching your target audience, there are two types of information you'll be putting together. The first is called *demographics*. Technically, it's the statistical study of populations. Demographics is the easy part. That data answers the questions *What, When,* and *Where.*

This is info that's readily available about people's external data. That is, things like where they live, how they commute, how much they make, their age, their race, and so forth. You can generally put this part of your profile together without directly asking people about themselves. While I always recommend getting your information directly from your existing contacts (a nice, friendly conversation over coffee or lunch works great), this type of information is aggregated by government agencies. You'd be surprised at how much detailed information the Post Office has on the people within their delivery routes! The Census bureau also collects all sorts of data. Start your search at www.census.gov .

In gathering demographic information about your target market, you want to grab as much information as possible. Once you gather all this information, you want to look for areas where the information for each person overlaps, where it's the same. Those are the areas where marketing messages will have the most impact.

A quick story: during WWII, Hungarian-born mathematician Abraham Wald started putting together pictures of planes that came back from missions, plotting the bullet holes in the planes. He stated that where the bullet holes did not appear was where additional armor should be placed on planes going out. Why? If a plane came back with bullet holes in a particular place, it was a good bet that a hole there wasn't going to stop the plane. But in places where there were no bullet holes, planes did not make it back. A bullet there probably shot down the plane. My point: there are two types of information we gather about customers - the data points that *seem* important (the bullets that hit the plane), and the data points that *are* important (the bullet holes you don't see because they brought down the plane).

What types of demographic questions do you want to ask? Here's a beginning list.

Country:
Region:
Urban or rural:
Age:
Race:
Own or rent:
Marital status:
Number of children at home:
Combined household income:

Religious affiliation:

What they buy from you:

What they don't buy that you offer:

Just by gathering answers to these questions, you'll begin to see your target market take shape. You might begin to plot their location on a physical map, or you might be able to draw a picture of them standing in front of their home. You can begin to predict what they buy from you, and how often.

This information will begin to give you a very broad picture of your current clients. But the picture it gives is very superficial. Think of walking down a city street and seeing a person. Let's say it's a woman, wearing a business suit and frowning. You cannot say what she wears every day, if she frowns all the time, or if she's going someplace new or habitual. It's a picture frozen in time, and doesn't tell you about her as a person, as an individual.

Our next chapter will help you gather that type of information.

Psychographics

According to Jairo Senise, psychographics is the study of personality, values, opinions, attitudes, interests, and lifestyles. This is the type of information we need to collect about our existing customers that will help us find people similar to them. If we look at information from our "best" (whatever that means to you) customer and find similarities, we can target people like them. Information about our "worst" customers can help us steer clear of people like them.

Don't just make up the data. If you already have one or more great clients that you'd like to duplicate, interview them. If you're searching for a target market, interview possible members of a group you want to target.

Here are some of the questions I like to ask that will yield psychographic information:

Top three personal interests:
Top three business interests:
Top three recreational interests:
Daily activities:
Hobbies:
What makes them happy:

What makes them sad:

What makes them angry:

What one thing would they add to their life:

What one thing would they remove from their life:

Daily commute:

Attitudes on religion:

Attitudes on politics:

What media they consume:

Daily time spent working:

Daily time spent on recreation:

Daily time spent on hobbies:

Daily time spent on family:

Daily time spent on other:

Where they shop:

What they shop for:

How they dress:

Food they like:

Food they don't like:

What vehicles they own:

What keeps them up at night:

What gets them out of bed in the morning:

Who they admire:

Who they hate:

To what they aspire:

As you'll see, this information cannot be gotten from existing pools of collected information. It must be gotten by asking an individual for their feelings and opinions. However, the answers to each question may overlap, especially the more answers you get.

This type of customer research can be very intrusive if done the wrong way and can make people uncomfortable or angry. It's best to explain to the people you're talking with that the questions will indeed be personal, and while you'd like them to answer honestly, it's okay if they skip questions that they don't want to answer. With demographic information, we know what they buy and don't buy from us. Here, we're trying to determine why and why not.

You might ask, *"I'm selling high-end widgets. Why do I want to ask a customer what kind of food they like to eat?"* My somewhat obtuse answer is: you never know how important the answer is until you ask the question. Honestly, it probably doesn't matter what the answer is to a particular question with any given individual. You're looking for commonalities of feeling and habit between members of the group. If you find that 67% of your existing customers like Italian food, you might set up a presentation at a good local Italian restaurant for prospects. You could guess that about 67% of them will have a positive attitude toward you before you even begin because they like Italian food.

There are several other categories we want to look at before attempting to put together our avatar.

Media and Entertainment

It really doesn't matter what system you're using as a sales model - business to business, business to consumer, network marketing, or any other. You should understand all the media that your prospects consume and what they do for entertainment. You'll begin to see common places you and your products/services can be tripped over, and if you understand the medium and why your prospects are there, you can begin to frame your marketing messages.

There are still a great number of industry magazines and blogs available out there, regardless of your business or niche. They exist because people read them - or watch them in the case of video outlets, or listen to them if we're talking about podcasts. But most people aren't consumed by what they do to earn a living. They like to spend time being entertained, and there are a million ways to spend your down time.

There are sports you watch and sports you play. There are solo hobbies and group hobbies. There are movies, plays, bars, restaurants, and shopping malls. I could make a three-page list and not get anywhere near close to describing even half the interests people have to get away from work.

Profile Your Target Market

An important point: even if you're selling products/services "b2b" (business to business), understanding what a prospective buyer is like away from work is vitally important. Remember, a business may *pay* for your products/services, but it's a person who *buys* them. We want to understand the person who buys us (and yes, they buy the seller first and the product/service second) so that we can understand what motivates similar people to buy.

At one time, watching sales presentations was a type of entertainment. Before radio and TV, you'd see throngs of people crowded around a huckster on a street corner. The salesperson wasn't only expected to explain the features and benefits of what they were selling, but to provide entertainment as well. Entertainment doesn't just cover the feelings of happiness and delight. Think about movies that make us cry, make us angry, depress us, or lift us up. Good entertainment can be cathartic - it purges us of negative feelings by guiding us through them. Understanding what emotions people feel and how they react to various stimuli can help us craft laser focused - and ultimately effective - marketing messages.

A half hour watching prime time network TV programming can prove very enlightening if you pay attention to the advertising. Very often, the ads attempt to couch their messages in a humorous presentation. Often the ad is not about the features and benefits (f&b) of what's being sold but about the feelings they want to associate with the product or service. Often advertisers will want to associate "the warm 'n fuzzies" with their product - a happy feeling you supposedly get when you experience their product.

These are the feelings people are searching for with their entertainment. It's important to keep that in mind.

The media they consume is often used in its capacity for entertainment as well, although it doesn't have to be viewed that way. These media can include websites, blogs, podcasts, TV programs, YouTube channels, and print magazines and newspapers - almost anything. Notice that not all of these things are part of the traditional "mass media." Narrow focus blogs and podcasts are part of what are called "micromedia." These are generally small circulation outlets, created more from passion than an attempt to create an advertising medium, that cater to an equally passionate audience. **NOTE:** *Nothing says that you can't create a similar micromedium for your target audiences!*

If prospects are consuming a particular medium or type of entertainment on a regular basis, this is definitely a place you should consider putting a message that can be tripped over!

Food

Once again, we come to the subject of food. Food is inextricably tied to who we are as a particular group of people. Just think of the different "types" of restaurants out there: Chinese, Italian, Middle Eastern, South American, etc. Those are all based on the "nationality" of the cuisine offered. You might also select a restaurant because it serves vegetarian food, or steaks, or chicken. You might go to a breakfast joint at night or a place that serves barbecued foods. You can also go to tea shops, coffee shops, and donut shops.

For most of the population of the United States, the food we prefer to consume says quite a great deal about us. It binds us within communities. Our dining situations are also telling - the Pennsylvania Dutch serve food in "family dining" situations, with everyone seated around a common table and passing large bowls and plates from person to person. Some people listen to music, others to educational programs, and others prefer just conversation. Some people prefer a quiet and reflective mealtime.

Before the food industry's massive output of prepared food in the latter part of the 20th century, the evening meal was a major focus of family time. Housewives spent all day shopping for and preparing the food they served to their family each day. Prepared foods, and often complete meals, freed up an enormous amount of time for the harried housekeeper.

Households went from single earner to dual earner. Since there was no one home to prepare meals, restaurants became busier and busier as people opted to have others prepare, serve, and clean up. As a child in the late 60s and 70s, I remember the few times I was treated to a meal in a restaurant. It was an occasion, usually celebrating some type of event. Now my wife and I go to restaurants 3 or 4 nights each week. She loves to cook, but she also enjoys being served a good meal.

Gathering for a meal can be an act of community. Generally, people choose the groups with whom they eat. Sometimes we go out to be alone with our significant other, and sometimes we're crammed in the back banquet room with other members of our group or association.

The groups in which we eat can tell a lot about our personalities, as can the types of food we eat, and where we consume it. It can be extremely important to get this type of information from our current and prospective clients, because interpreting the data can tell us so much about where and how to find members of our target market.

Family

Many times, we tend to think of "family" as a group of people related by blood or marriage, and it can certainly fit that description. Regardless of negative situations like divorces, death, and abandonment, we tend to think of those people like cousins, siblings, parents, and children as the closest members of our family.

The word "family" can also be used metaphorically to create more inclusive categories such as community, nationhood, global village, and humanism. Many people will argue that their family is made up of people with whom they share similar values and outlooks, not those with whom they share legal or blood ties. They will tell you that their family is made up of the people they choose to be with, the people to whom they feel closest and with whom they share emotional connections.

We tend to share things within and among our family. Some of these are tangible, like clothing and cheese. Many are intangible like information, opinions, and feelings. Family can influence our views and perceptions like almost no other group.

When you're profiling your current or prospective customers, it's important to try to understand their families and how those groups of people influence one another. In some families one or two people express their views on a particular situation and everyone goes along with it. In other families, topics are discussed among the members and a consensus is reached. There are almost as many patterns of interaction as there are types of people in families.

In addition to trying to reach prospects with your message, you should consider how your messages will be seen and passed on by other members of the family. Remember, family members may be members of the same target market you're attempting to reach. *Ideally, your best salesperson is a customer that's thrilled with your products or services.* If they don't need to reach very far to turn an acquaintance into one of your customers, that's a bonus for everyone.

The idea is to influence your prospect's group of influences - in this case, their family - in a positive manner. That will make it much easier to grab the attention of your target market.

Work

Even if you are selling products or services to people at their homes, it's important to understand where they work, what they do, and with whom they have business relationships. Knowing these things can give you important clues about what your marketing messages should be and where to place them for maximum impact.

To return to my sports car example, it may be that members of my target market all work in similar industries or even at the same company. Finding one person who has social influence with others can facilitate several sales. Larry may buy one of my cars, and when co-workers Pete and Jim see it, they ask Larry where he got it, and they come in for test drives.

Of course, you may find that your target market is *not* influenced on a daily basis by the people with whom they work. If you recall my story about the bullet holes in the airplanes, it's important to understand what *seems to be* important and separate that information from *what truly is* important.

On the other hand, people whom we work with day in and day out can be highly influential to our views. Some people are friends, some acquaintances, and others enemies. Some we don't think about at all. Understanding how closely our prospects work with others and what kinds of tasks they do that overlap can help you understand what messages they're ready to hear and where you can place those messages.

Take myself as an example. A bad example, I'll admit. My staff is spread out across the US. I often work alone, from home or some remote location with Internet access. My most frequent means of interaction is email, with shared document editing coming in second. I speak with my clients on the phone infrequently, but usually on group calls. I have a number of people I consider "business acquaintances" and we do share influence on certain subjects back and forth, but if you were trying to sell me a new computer (which I currently need), trying to reach me through my work contacts would be almost futile.

Asking questions of your current or prospective clients, it's important to uncover how they interact with work colleagues, and in what areas they influence each other.

Why Do You Buy?

Throughout this book, I've been telling you to directly ask your current and prospective customers the questions to which you want answers. I'm about to do it again.

Among my own clients, I find that they were initially reluctant to do this. I suppose I was too at one point, but I can't tell you why. Perhaps it was a fear of hearing negative feedback or fear of looking like a fool. I simply don't remember. At this point, I look forward to the very enlightening answers I get and putting that information to use building better relationships with my clients and prospects.

Here's a question you must ask of your best clients: *Why do you buy what you do from me?* And its follow up: *Why don't you buy the other things which you could buy from me?*

It's nearly impossible to build a compelling marketing message to attract people similar to your best clients *if you don't understand why they buy from you.* This is vital information, and I find most small businesses just don't ask these questions.

If you don't know that people only buy blue widgets from you because you don't carry red ones, you're missing out not only on information but sales as well. How many more prospects could you sell to if you added red widgets? How would you know that you're missing those sales if you didn't ask customers about what they buy or prospects about what they want to buy?

After you ask these questions, you must apply what I call *The FUFT Principle*. That is, **Follow Up, Follow Through**. Once your customer or prospect tells you why they buy or don't buy your products/services, you need to Follow Up with relevant questions. I can't tell you exactly what those questions are because they will be based on what people tell you, but they could include: What would you buy if we offered it? What do you buy from others that you'd like a better version of? What can we offer you that will help you do business?

Once you have answers to those questions, don't drop the ball! Now you need to Follow Through - research the ways you can help the customer or prospect based on their answers and most importantly, keep them informed. *"Hey Suzie, remember when I asked you about buying those red widgets? We're currently evaluating suppliers, and we'll let you know pricing and delivery as soon as we have that info."*

I have a Thai restaurant as a client. He assumed it was his food that was drawing in regulars week after week. Then, I asked his customers. They told me the food was good, but it was the owner's friendly attitude that drew them back. Many other restaurants in the area (regardless of their specialty) had staff that simply took their customers' orders and didn't interact with them. My client's family shared their stories with customers, and made them feel included and valued. Rather than add dishes to the menu to increase sales, he had his family spend more time with customers, and suggest appetizers and desserts. Sales went up, and both he and his customers were still happy.

By understanding what makes your current customers happy with you, you can then build marketing messages that reach the same type of people with that information. You're building your target market by understanding what makes people happy to do business with you and telling others how they'll be happy too.

Building the Avatar

Once you have interviewed several of your best customers and people who are perhaps some of your better prospects, you need to start compiling the answers to your questions.

I mentioned the WWII planes, remember? It's not the holes you see that are important; it's the holes you don't see. When I'm considering buying something online, I look at the reviews. I don't really care about the 5 star, "It's great!!!" reviews. I look for negative reviews. Specifically, I look for detailed negative reviews (1 and 2 star reviews) that explain exactly what the person didn't like. Negative reviews like, "This sucks" tell me nothing about the product/service or about the author.

Regardless of how detailed the answers about "Why I love doing business with you," I generally lump them all together as a positive answer to that question. For the purpose of building a profile of our avatar, you don't need to enumerate all the ways people love you, your products, and your services. It's enough to know they've given you positive answers to those questions. Why they love you or why they hate you is, for the moment, irrelevant. However, don't throw those answers away! They can help you modify your procedures so that you can meet the needs of other prospects later, giving you more ways to please your target market.

One good way of doing this is to build a database of the questions and all the answers. (You can do this ahead of time - design your questions and put them in a database, and then enter the answers for people as you interview them.) Then, look at the answers to each question and add up the number of answers that are the same for each question, positive or negative. Do you have a suggestion for a particular database or a number of people to survey?

It's important that you're not just looking at people you consider your best prospects or customers. It's also important to gather information from people who are not good customers. Try to get them all to open up and elaborate on their answers, either positive or negative.

Back in the 1970s, there was a show called *The White Shadow*. In one segment, the school principal sat down with a student and gave her this advice:

"There are four kinds of people in our lives: people who like us for the right reasons, people who like us for the wrong reasons, people who don't like us for the right reasons, and people who don't like us for the wrong reasons. The two groups you need to worry about are the people who like you for the wrong reasons, and people who don't like you for the right reasons." (*Visit AgileMarketingServices.com and search the blog for White Shadow for a longer explanation.*)

While this is true, and you want to address those issues at a later date, in order to build our avatar we're just looking for answers that match from person to person.

Here's an example of the bullets/no bullets pictures I was talking about earlier. Let's say you get 20 different people to give you answers to all your psychographic questions. One question is, *"What media do you consume?"* Among the answers, you get 6 people who tell you "Trade periodicals" and 4 people who answer, "Other." You can put all those people in one group if you want, but you should go back and ask all of them the follow-up question, *"Exactly which media do you read/listen to/watch?"*

You'll use the answers to the follow-up questions to figure out where exactly their interests and attention coincide.

Painting the Picture

Now that you've collected all sorts of information from your best and worst clients, and perhaps from prospective customers, it's time to start painting the picture of your avatar.

We'll think of it as a picture because, like the frowning woman in a business suit we mentioned a few chapters back, it's just a snapshot of an idealized person and his/her life. But it's a word picture, a written description of our ultimate customer. It's a picture of who they are, how they live, and why they buy - or should buy - your products and services.

This does not have to be a literary masterpiece. Don't worry about spelling, grammar, or stringing ideas together into a compelling story. This word picture is for internal business use only, for your use in trying to figure out who your average target market member is.

You're going to look at all the answers you got to your demographic and psychographic questions, specifically searching for answers that overlap. No, everyone doesn't live in the same house, but maybe many people live in an affluent suburb or a housing development with large families. Maybe you've got a mix of male and female prospects, but most of them own at least one dog. You're looking for statistical similarities.

Don't let the term "statistical" worry you. It's just a fancy way of saying you're going to be counting up similar answers and comparing them. Let's say you get 100 answers to the question, "What type of recreational activity do you enjoy?" You might put together a list like this:

> Going to the movies = 25
> Visiting the state park = 17
> Roller skating = 6
> Baking = 3
> Opera = 2
> Other = 47

The top three answers make up almost half the answers you received. So does "other," but that includes 47 different answers, everything from "reading" to "walking the dog" and "visiting a nursing home." The top two answers cover the recreational habits of over 40% of the respondents. These answers are statistically significant. When you write up a description of your avatar, you can say they entertain themselves by either going to movies or visiting the state park.

When you write up your avatar profile, use whatever format works for you. If it's a long, flowery description, that's great. If it's a bare list of attributes, that's fine, too. You can mix the two if you want. The object is to keep the profile in mind when you're deciding where your marketing will appear, in what format, and how you want to present the message. You'll want to build the profile using all the answers that are statistically meaningful. Like the "movies & park" answers above, it's okay if you mention 2 or 3 answers for a particular question, as long as they're the top answers. For instance, you wouldn't want to mention "roller skating" since only six of our imaginary customers said that.

Let me give you two examples for the same person. Again, either one is valid. It's not about the format; it's about creating a profile you find useful. Here are a couple different versions for the Zeta Zipper target market.

****

Larry is a 57-year-old divorced white male. His daughter is in her final year of undergraduate university. Last year he moved from a small, cheap apartment into an upscale apartment complex about a 20-minute drive from work.

Larry is a vice president at the local office of a company that has locations on the east coast of the US, and in Canada. With salary and bonuses, he makes just under $150k/year. Since his divorce 10 years ago, a lot of his disposable income has gone towards child support on tuition. Larry is a big believer in saving for retirement, though. He's been leasing newer but inexpensive cars for the last nine years.

Larry is politically moderately conservative, and a non-practicing Catholic, although he gives small donations to faith-based charities.

While most people in his office listen to a local FM radio station, he has a satellite radio subscription for his office and car, where he mostly listens to 60's and 70's music.

He's been thinking about taking a tropical vacation, but he's not ready to spring for one yet. However, long weekends where he can drive to his destination are something he's decided he's ready to do.

Larry has had dreams his whole life of long sunny drives in a top-down sports car. He's been doing research. He wants something sporty, but economical. He's been doing this research mostly online. He's looking to buy a car this time, one that will last until he's about ready to retire.

His company is doing well, but Larry knows he's got a title other people – younger people – want. Part of the reason he works out is to keep up his energy and younger appearance. He also wants to attract a younger woman as a girlfriend and potential travel companion. Besides working out at the gym, he also goes to sports bars a couple times each month with buddies from college, and he reads biography books at home or at a local coffee house. He likes print books, but also has a Kindle ereader.

Larry is also on the lookout for fun destinations he can drive to in his new sports car. Places the famous people he reads about in his biographies lived, worked, or did something else famous.

****

Name: Larry
Age: late 50s
Race: Caucasian
Location: Upscale suburban apartment
Pets: None

Job: VP at local office of east coast company

Politics: Moderate conservative

Religion: Lapsed Catholic

Desires: Freedom, dream fulfilment, hot girlfriend to travel with

Worries: Losing his job before he's ready

Goals: Buy a sports car, long weekend drives, be economical

Aspirations: To have a hot girlfriend beside him as they travel down the road, top down, with the wind in their hair.

Recreation: Working out at gym, a few hours at sports bar with friends, oldies music, reading biographies

Media: Businessweek magazine, local online news sites, satellite radio

****

See? Very similar. Some of you will like the first version, and some will find that the second version makes you happy. Both describe the same aggregate person. Neither is better than the other. All that matters is being able to use the avatar to help you make marketing decisions.

Using Your Target Market Avatar

Once you've written out your avatar's profile, how do you use it? That's the $64 question!

We need to circle back around to our original reasons for asking questions and putting together the profile. We wanted to understand who our best prospects were, where to find them, and what they wanted to hear from us.

The first and easiest thing we might find out from the profile is where our best prospects live and hang out. If we're wildlife photographers, we can't take pictures of a specific animal if we don't know where and how they live. Let's use our example avatar, Larry. We know our best target market members are higher level employees making over $100k/year. They live in higher-end but affordable housing, and may be going through what's laughing called a "mid-life crisis." They have a car currently, but are looking for a sporty ride for themselves and a friend.

Because we know where they live, what they do to socialize, and how they get around, we can begin to understand where to put our messages so that our prospects might trip over them.

Based on the answers to some of our psychographic questions, we begin to understand the worries that keep them up at night, and the reasons they get up in the morning. Because of this, we can frame our messages so that they address the concerns our prospects already have. Larry is worried about feeling and appearing young; for his subordinates, his superiors, and younger ladies he could end up dating. Depending on what information we want to pass along, this gives us several points to enter into a conversation with him and the tone we want to use when addressing him.

Our avatar profile also tells us about the media Larry reads, watches, and listens to. With this information, we can begin to adjust our advertising so that we appear in front of him (and the rest of our target market members) as often as possible with the messages that are important to them, using language that resonates with them.

All of the information we've gathered is important. If we know anything about our target market's social life and family life, we might find a way to insert ourselves there. If it's relevant, we might begin an association with large organizations in their life where we can complement what's already going on. We might choose to appear at the places they buy food - markets and restaurants. Or if our messages are deeper, perhaps the places they worship.

Using the avatar helps us decide where and when we place our messages, and the language and media we use to present them. If we know what causes them pain, perhaps we can do something to relieve it. Perhaps we can create content that makes them happy, gives them some kind of pleasure.

The avatar profile should help you understand what your target market members want from you and how to get it to them.

Who Is Like Your Avatar?

We surveyed a number of current and prospective customers, then took their answers and looked for commonalities. We took those similar answers and put together an aggregate personality from those answers to describe ideal members of our target market.

Now, from that description, we're going to extrapolate out and look for people who fit that idealized profile as closely as possible.

If your business serves local customers, the first part is easy. You look for people in the area where your avatar "lives." Maybe it's a section of a city or a suburb. Maybe it's a zip code or even a USPS delivery route. If your product/service is general enough, maybe it's a county, a region, or even a state.

Or, let's look for people who match your avatar physically. You want to focus on age and gender, race, and any other physical aspects that are important parts of your product/service. For instance, if you're marketing a salon, you're probably looking for women who like to get their hair styled on a regular basis. "Styling" may include washing, cutting, and coloring, so you're looking to match all of those aspects of a woman's desires.

It may not be "polite" to discuss, but you want to consider how much money your target market has and how they'll pay you. Will your sale be an emergency purchase put on a credit card? Will it be something your prospect saves up for? Will prospects need to take out a loan? Is your product/service something they pay for with pocket money? By considering the cost to them and how your prospects will be paying, you may learn something about them as a group. It might help you find them physically or to reach target market members within larger groups.

An important aspect is what your avatar does for fun. You'll want to look at similar general recreation activities and think about how you can reach members of your target market. For instance, not everyone goes to an art museum for the same reasons. Some people visit every weekend with their children. Others are artists themselves and go to study the art installed there. Others may bring groups to the museum on a regular basis, but don't pay much attention to the art. Not everyone visits a recreational area for the same reasons. You should examine the reasons your avatar visits these places.

Not all features of your avatar are equally important. It all depends on what products/services you're marketing. I have one client who actually wound up creating two different products. Her first info product was written for people with a graduate-level education. Her original target market, which we called *Walmart Moms*, would not have been able to understand it, so she re-crafted the book using much simpler language. After she was done, she had essentially the same product aimed at two different target market groups. In this case it wasn't age, gender, or income that was the differentiating factor; it was their literacy level.

While the profile is important, it shouldn't hold you to a rigid format. Although our example avatar, Larry, is a white male in his mid- to late-fifties, depending on the product or service I'm promoting, talking with an African American woman in her 30s might be equally valid. Once you create a profile, you should decide which aspects are the most important and focus on those first to find more members of your target market. Then you can become more flexible on how closely real people match your profile as you work your way down the list.

It's important to look at the profile you've written and try to figure out a way to put yourself, your business, and your products/services somewhere on a pathway your prospects use so that they have a chance to trip over you. The "path" might be a physical one (like buying ads on busses and subways prospects use) or it might be a mental space they occupy. That's the point of using an avatar's profile - finding places and ways to be tripped over and to create connections with members of your target market.

Where Do You Find Them?

Let's imagine for a few minutes that you're a photographer - specifically, a wildlife photographer from our earlier example. You decide you want to take a picture of a deer. If you're in North America, you travel to the area between the Rocky Mountains and Columbia Mountains in Canada where all 5 indigenous species - white-tailed deer, mule deer, caribou, elk, and moose - can be found together. If you're on the East Coast, you'll find white-tailed deer in the woods. If you're west of the Missouri River, you'll likely be snapping pix of mule deer.

Let me say something that will sound kind of stupid: No matter what kind of deer you're looking for, you are 99.9% unlikely to find them standing in the middle of a busy intersection of a city at noon.

Another stupid statement: Standing in the middle of a field and taking a picture does not guarantee you'll be getting a deer of any kind in the shot. Again, given a random assortment of fields and times of day, I'd say it's 99.9% certain you won't be taking a picture with a deer in it.

If I'm selling my Zeta Zipper 2-seater expensive sports car, getting a list of random people in no way guarantees that one of those people will buy a car from me.

Deer live in the woods, not in the middle of cities. We know this about them. They also wander around fairly large areas, living their lives. If it's fall and there's an apple tree with fruit falling to the ground, there's a good chance that some deer will wander by at some point to eat.

Now, rabbits are much smaller. They don't need as much area to live their rabbity lives. You can wander a much smaller area of woods or fields and have a good chance of finding several rabbit families.

For squirrels, you don't even have to leave the city. You might find them at the busiest intersection of the city, scampering across power lines, up and down trees, and darting between cars.

The point is, if you know what allows an animal to live its life, you can figure out the habitat where it might be found. If you go there at the right time of day for the animal to be out and about, you'll probably get your pictures. Knowing what they eat and the kind of lives they like to live can help you find them.

The same is true of the people who make up your target market. One of the reasons you're gathering all the information about and from them is to learn as much as you can about them as a group. Are they single young adults living in the city center? Are they mid-thirties heads of families living in the suburbs? Matrons of farm families living in the rural stretches between Midwestern towns? Remember, you want to put your marketing message where your target market will trip over it. If they live on farms and listen to country music, putting an ad on an urban hip hop radio station will not reach them.

You want to match your message, and the medium in which it appears, to the environment where you'll find the people you want as customers. Now, I'm not necessarily talking about the physical location of the individuals, although in the examples so far in this chapter, I've been talking about cities and farms.

If the target market for my sports car is a man with no kids at home and at least $100,000 dollars in the bank, I'm more likely to find him by looking at what kind of media he consumes, rather than by what his zip code is. I have a better chance of him tripping over my marketing in a particular magazine, rather than on a particular billboard at the side of a particular road.

But if my target market for another product is young urban girls, I'm going to buy ads on bus stops and in subways in major cities. I have to know where to find the people I want to trip over my messages, whether it's a physical location, a shared medium they consume, or a common recreation event.

You need to look at not just the demographic information you've gathered, but the psychographic info as well and figure out the common intersection points for a majority of the prospects and clients. Where will most of them have a common chance of encountering your message? And what's the most common internal conversation that you can enter?

What Are Their Pressure Points?

In getting to know your target market members, you need to find out the things that bother them. Sometimes these are referred to as "pain points." Other people call them "stress points." I sometimes call these "itches that need scratching," because not all the points that require attention are painful - that is, not attending to them won't cause systems to slow or stop. Another term, which we'll use in this book, is "pressure point." Pressure points on the human body can trigger pain or numbness. They can also bring on pleasure and relief. It all depends on how you rub them and how strongly.

Whatever you call them, these are specific areas in your target market's lives that are distracting them from their daily lives. These areas keep people from accomplishing as much as they'd like. If you've got a product or service that will alleviate one or more of those distractions, the happier they'll be to do business with you. The more relief or pleasure you bring to their lives, the more they'll be able to tolerate higher prices.

As much as we tend to believe it, money is **not** the first pressure point for most people. The solution to every problem is not a lower price. If you think about it, all you have to do to replace lost money is to work more hours or sell more products or services. In the scheme of things, lost money is fairly easy to replace.

With respect to Mark Twain and Will Rogers, "Buy land - they're not making any more of it" is a good try, but not entirely accurate. Time, however, is extremely finite. Every hour, every minute, every *second* that passes is impossible to get back. Some people don't value it the same as other people do. We spend a lot of time trying to manage time, hold back the effects of time. No matter if it's a fleeting wish or a heartfelt prayer, we cannot go back and change our actions or jump ahead to see how some other action turns out. And while I'd say some aspect of "more time" underlays perhaps 75% of your target market's pressure points, it's also not the only "itch" out there.

I can't begin to tell you what pressure points your target market members have in common. If you're selling cars, I'd guess that almost everyone who buys a new car needs one - or at least, they want one and can afford it. But I can tell you this: it may not be the relief of a direct pressure point that causes a sale. For instance, you may sell a car to someone who wants his/her kid to get back and forth to college on the other end of the state. A car for the child is one solution, but not the *only* one. A public transportation pass and airline tickets are other possibilities. The car's purpose may not be solely to transport the student; it may also serve to carry supplies back and forth or other such purposes.

Asking direct questions of your customers and prospects is always a great idea. "What motivated you to buy this from us? What itch did this scratch?" However, some people don't know why they do things. Some prevaricate as a matter of course. Some people think their motivation is X when it's really Y. It may be difficult to get to the true reason they buy, but their answer is always the best place to start.

I was asked to submit a proposal to a small town once. I showed up with a pad and pen to my appointment. My contact person was initially perplexed.

"Where's your equipment? Aren't you going to put on a slideshow or something? Aren't you going to give me a presentation?"

"About what?" I asked. "I can't propose a solution to a problem I know nothing about."

It turns out that every other marketing firm - all six that responded to his solicitation - had produced a presentation based on what they assumed he needed. Not one had bothered to ask questions, even of his secretary, about what the town needed. Sad to say, I was the only person who tried to understand what the development committee wanted before putting on a dog and pony show. Happily for me, I got the contract.

If you can, building relationships with your target market members is a huge help. Not only for you, but for them as well. Buying a widget from someone you know and trust ultimately provides more satisfaction than buying the same thing from "some company." They know (or hope or imagine) that the person with whom they have a relationship is going to treat them better than a random person selling the same thing. It's ultimately easier to go to a person who you know and believe in, who knows about your pressure points, than it is to pick some person off the street to sell you what you need.

The deeper the relationship becomes between you and your clients and prospects, the more they'll share about their pressure points. The better you understand them, the better chance you have of offering a solution that can help them.

What Internal Conversation Can You Join?

People don't exist in a bubble or vacuum. Your clients and prospects have pressure points (see the previous chapter) they want massaged, itches they want scratched. They're already having conversations with others and with themselves about those issues. Your object in crafting your marketing messages is to join the flow of that internal conversation as effortlessly as possible.

But how do you know what those conversations might be? As I've said, they're mostly internal. Most folks don't wander the streets sharing their hopes and worries. *(For those of you interested in the folks that **do** wander the streets muttering to themselves, please talk with my wife. She's a psychologist, and she's looking for the topic to her next book.)* So how do you find out what they're thinking about?

I always recommend asking and then listening to the replies you get. Engage your existing customers and your prospects in light conversation, asking them about themselves. No need to get heavy: *Tell me exactly what pains keep you up at night.* At least, not at first. Like all other relationships, some remain superficial, others get deep, and most remain somewhere in between.

Many businesses and entrepreneurs think communicating is talking to customers and prospects. It's not. It's talking *with* people. It's getting feedback from them. It's providing them with talking prompts and discussion sparks and letting them talk. If people know you're listening to them, they'll be more likely to listen to you. When you listen to people, you know what they want to hear. By listening to what people are saying, you know what their internal conversations are and you can craft your marketing messages to match those conversations.

There are many different ways to engage with people. Advertising - paid messages appearing in someone else's media - is one way. But there are other ways to have a two-way conversation. Think of magazines and newspapers; they often have a "letters to the editor" section. Print and email newsletters are great. Podcasts, whether video or audio, are marvelous ways to respond to comments and questions. You can address evergreen questions and comments – ones that come up over and over again - any time. Any other discussions should be handled as soon as they're brought up, otherwise you lose the opportunity to engage in that internal conversation.

The pressure points people experience are opportunities for you. Either you have a chance to solve their problems or at least learn what their problems are. Understanding people is important. Blundering in with the wrong words, the wrong emotions, is worse than missing the opportunity completely.

Pain is one side of the coin. Pleasure is the other side. Some internal conversations are not about "What's rubbing me the wrong way." Many people are thinking about, "I want something that makes me happy." You want to determine which conversation you have the best chance of entering. Some people are better at crafting "pain" messages than they are "pleasure" messages, and vice versa. That's fine, but you should attempt to be ready for either. Many people are thinking about both tracks at once.

There are other pressure points as well, but these are the two main points of entry for most marketers.

Talk to the Individual

When the time comes where you're putting together your marketing message, don't try to be a professional. A lot of business owners and entrepreneurs start to write their messages like they think they should be written: in a formal, stilted way that tries to impart a message to a whole group. Please don't do that.

I used to do that myself. A lot of the copy I wrote (and that people paid for!) as a young marketer was non informational, wordy crap. If you write your message for a group, it will totally pass over the heads of individuals.

The whole point of building an avatar is to allow you to talk directly to the avatar. You address that one person as if you know him/her, because you do. You've spent time finding out what the avatar is interested in, and because the avatar's hopes and fears are a combination of the hopes and fears of real people, then when your message addresses those things, you're talking individually to hundreds or even thousands of people at once.

I've used the example of a car dealer selling an expensive sports car throughout the book. Let's take a look at a couple pieces of copy. We've decided that our target market likes the fact that they can drive

500 miles on a tank of gas, so that's the "itch" we're going to "scratch."

> *People enjoy driving the Zeta Zipper. They enjoy it so much that they just want to keep going and going. So we designed the car with a large tank. When you get on the highway, you can travel up to 500 miles without stopping for gas.*

This is text that certainly describes the benefit we're trying to get across. We've addressed it to "people" - a generic group if there ever was one. But it doesn't speak to an individual. It tells a group what they can expect from the car.

Now, let's say the same thing to our avatar, as if they were sitting across from us.

> *When you get behind the wheel of the Zeta Zipper, you're gonna love it. And you won't have to hunt for a gas station every hour, either. That big gas tank will let you keep the wind in your hair on the back roads from New York City to Charlotte, North Carolina.*

The first thing you should notice is that I'm now talking to "you." I address the person directly. Next, I'm no longer going by the book with my spelling and grammar. I've intentionally used a non-standard contraction - gonna - instead of trying to keep my language prim and proper. I can also talk about "wind in your hair" because I'm not trying to be polite to bald men and make them feel included. I'm giving a concrete example of driving distance, and since this ad will run (let's pretend) in the NYC market, I've started the trip from there and mentioned a specifically aspirational drive.

As we've said before, you want to enter the conversation that's already going on in the heads of your target market members. Here, I'm addressing the question, "If I had this car, where would I drive to?" I'm telling them about the mileage they'll get on one tank and suggesting a trip (and describing one of the joys - wind in your hair) on back roads, not highways.

In that example, I was addressing a pleasure point - what will make the customer happy. But you can speak directly to the person's fears as well.

> *You could imagine the worst when your teenager keeps the family car out past curfew. Eliminate your uncertainty by installing KarTrakker so you know where your car is at all times.*

You don't beat around the bush with your friends. They say something stupid and you call them on it. They say they're worried and you reassure them. You don't take 10 minutes to justify what you're about to say. It's exactly the same thing with your marketing messages. You listen to their hopes and fears and address those things directly. You don't worry about grammar too much. Just be clear enough to get your message across to the individual to whom you're speaking. And yes, I intentionally used proper, complex grammar in that last sentence. You noticed it, didn't you? Hehe!

Profile Your Target Market

Connecting Via Social Media

Some entrepreneurs and small business owners hear the phrase "social media marketing" and default to the idea of running advertising on Twitter, Instagram, or Facebook, all of which you can do, and have it turn out all right, if you run it through their ad systems. Unfortunately, some folks start posting 100% ads in their feeds.

This is a *fast* way to get ignored or even banned by your connections. The only people who will want to connect with you at that point are people trying to sell you things - either their own products and services "guaranteed to drive buyers through your doors" - or people who are just as clueless about using social media.

The most important thing to remember about social media is that it's called **social** media for a reason. This is where people hang out and relax, let their hair down and talk about things that are important to them. Just a quick browse of a site like Facebook and you'll see posts about children, sports, concerts, exercise, video games, school, significant others - I could go on and on. There are almost no posts about "Where can I buy. . ." or "who makes the best..."

Social media can be anywhere. Today when we use that phrase, we're often talking about web sites that promote interaction between people based on shared interests or social groups. This perfectly describes the stereotypical "general store" of ages past. I know many people who "hang out" in diners late into the night, interacting with people in their group, the staff, and others who come in for food or coffee. When you question your customers and prospects, find out where they hang out - in real life or virtually - and in what groups, to relax.

Imagine one of these groups sitting together and talking in a diner. Suddenly, a man dressed in a suit comes in and insistently starts telling members of the group why they need to buy a car from him and why they need to do it now. He's an interruption, a bother. They are at minimum going to ignore him. If he becomes too much of a nuisance, they'll ask the staff to kick him out. And that's the mistake that many people make when they hear the phrase, "social media marketing."

The best tactic here is to join the discussion as a friendly participant, sharing help or comments on the topics that come up. Occasionally, if the subject comes up, you can gently offer your services.

Let's go back to our social group at the diner. Now a new gentleman comes in, dressed in casual clothes. He listens to ongoing conversations, making comments and observations when appropriate. One night, during a conversation about kids, one of the group members notes that his teenaged son just crashed the family car and they need to find a new one. The new gentleman casually mentions that he sells cars, passes over his card, and tells the other group member to call if he can help. And that's it - they go on to other topics.

Social media marketing is about contributing to ongoing conversations, not commandeering the discussion. Social media members make small talk about different subjects, sharing information with one another. *The real "marketing" that goes on is building relationships with members of the group.* Sometimes you build relationships by introducing yourself with your marketing messages. In this case, you build relationships by being friendly and helpful first, and then sharing your marketing messages when people have the need for them.

Not all marketing messages to your target market need to be sales related. A great deal of them, no matter where you put them, should be aimed at helping your target market with those pressure points, either relieving pain or helping give pleasure.

Make a Connection

Whether it's through some type of codified social media (web sites, live meetings, etc.) or not, your main focus should be building a connection with members of your target market. You need to establish a two-way communication first and use that to make a connection. Give them something first (see the next chapter, *Help First*).

As the saying goes, "They won't care how much you know, until they know how much you care."

I had a client who had an annual event for which he printed a program. He tried unsuccessfully to sell ad space and then hired my company to sell ads. When I reported that we'd only sold one, he was angry. I then asked him if he had any type of recognition program in place. He looked at me like I had three heads.

So we set up a simple Certificate of Appreciation program. Each certificate he gave out cost him less than $5 and half an hour of time. He picked people he did business with or who were simply neighboring businesses. He printed a certificate up with their name on it, presented it to them, and took a picture. He gave them a copy of the picture, and wrote a short press release about that company and submitted it. The next year, over 50% of the CofA recipients bought ads in his program. Demonstrating to other people that you think about them, especially when you're not trying to sell them something, has a huge impact.

This is where creating content - books, videos, blogs, newsletters, etc. - to massage your target market's pressure points becomes important. If you can create a free or low cost content product that will help them relieve a pain or give them pleasure, you have a chance of making a strong connection. But remember, a connection goes two ways. Solicit their feedback, ask them how their life is going, almost anything. By asking questions, and showing that you're listening to the answers, you'll build strong connections.

Once they know you're listening to them, you have a much better chance of getting them to listen to you when you send out a marketing message. When they do see it (or hear it), they'll be more likely to process it in a positive manner. That is, you have a better chance of them not being annoyed, or angry, or experiencing some other negative emotion when they see your ad or article. If you've got a track record of supplying them with info they can use, they might act on, and pass along, your message.

Help First

Once you determine who your target market is, where to reach them, and what their pressure points are, what should your first marketing message be?

A hand up.

All business owners and entrepreneurs think that they've got marvelous products and services, and if their target market only knew about them, they'd come running with cash in their hands. Sometimes that's true, but most often it isn't. We want to tell them how much easier and better their lives or businesses would be if they just bought our products and services. But please resist the urge.

We talked about making connections in the last chapter. The best connection is one where the other person knows you are willing to take away their pain or help them achieve pleasure. Most people want to do business with people they see as "good folks" - people who are willing to give first and sell later, people who have their best interest at heart.

I can't tell you I'm a good person and have you believe it. I can't get you to buy my widgets by telling you they're better than someone else's. But if you see it. . . if you trip over my qualities out there in the world, I have a better chance of you believing those things about me.

My friend Tom Shine of Horizon Productions (HorizonOnHold.com) told me years ago, "Make sure you're caught in the act of doing good." Part of that is offering a hand to those in need. This could be a free product or service that you sell or just some other form of assistance that someone might need. While you're doing this, there's generally nothing wrong with publicizing the act. Make sure there's a picture, or a video, and that the story comes to the attention of the right media.

That being said, your main reason for helping others should **not** be for notoriety or publicity. Giving out cheap gimcracks or offering meaningless help doesn't make you a hero or even a particularly nice person for that matter. But you don't have to run around pulling little old ladies out of burning buildings, either.

The main reward for doing good, at least in my book, is the warm and fuzzy feeling you get from helping others. But "help" could simply be info on how to avoid getting screwed over when buying a new car. Save people time or money or aggravation, and most of those folks will appreciate it.

If your target market is helped by your positive deeds or if they come to know of your good works, they'll be more receptive to developing a connection. Connections lead to relationships, and relationships lead to repeat sales.

So before you put out a marketing message, examine those pressure points and create a solution. Scratch an itch. Make it available for low or no cost, and make sure people in your target market know about it.

Build Your Avatar into Your Marketing Plan

You're going to spend a great deal of time and possibly money doing research and then writing up your target market avatar. Once you've done that first version, you need to plug it back into everything you're doing. One place that avatar is extremely important is in putting together your marketing plan.

When you're planning the steps you need to take to craft and share your marketing messages, you want to look at your avatar profile and all the compiled info around it. If you find that many of your best customers and prospects read one particular blog for their national news, you may want to spend a lot of your time and effort trying to get stories about you and your business placed there. You should also consider spending a chunk of your advertising budget there as well. If none of your interviewees has mentioned reading *Parade Magazine* like you do, you wouldn't want to spend money buying an ad there.

A few of my former clients have had favorite media. I mean, it's *their* favorite media, not their clients'. And those media are where they insisted on spending their ad budgets. In every case, it was a waste of cash. Remember my example of the wildlife photographer? You're not going to find a moose to take a picture of hanging around a street corner in a busy city. Make sure you're addressing your target market's pressure points and putting that content somewhere they will trip over it.

You want to plan everything around that avatar. Put your messages in the media they consume. Put ads and content in or near the entertainment venues where they hang out. Address their specific pressure points; relieve their pain and give them pleasure. You want to talk to them, engage them in a conversation. Ignore anyone who isn't part of your specific target market.

As tough as it might be, there will be certain messages and venues you'll want to bury. As they say: A good idea for a story is *not* the same as an idea for a good story – that is, a good idea doesn't guarantee a good outcome. You may have a great message that addresses a problem your target market just doesn't have. Somebody may give you a great deal on space in a medium your target market doesn't consume. To pursue those is a waste of your resources. If you don't have a good chance of getting your message to your target market, don't craft the content or spend the money. In order to sell Zeta Zippers, I'm not going to buy cheap ad space in a magazine about classic trucks. Yes, some people who collect classic trucks may have the money to buy my sports cars, but I'm going to guess they'd rather put that cash towards yet another rebuilt pickup.

All your efforts should be pointed in one direction. You want to connect with your target market as deeply as possible. You want to ask them questions and engage them in the conversation that's already happening inside their head. The only way that this is going to work is to put that avatar at the center of your marketing plan. Remember - ***laser focus***!

As an example, let's build what I call a Cocktail Napkin Marketing Plan. You might also call this an Executive Marketing Plan. It's short and to the point and makes a great place to start. You'll want to expand from here.

Your marketing plan should be able to fit on a cocktail napkin or small piece of paper. It will look like this:

The target market of ___(1)___ is ___(2)___. They work in ___(3)___. For entertainment, they enjoy ___(4)___, ___(5)___ and ___(6)___. The conversation in their head we want to enter is about ___(7)___. We can help them with the following things:

___(8)___ by ___(9)___
___(10)___ by ___(11)___
___(12)___ by ___(13)___

They can trip over us in the following ways:

In ___(14)___ with ___(15)___
In ___(16)___ with ___(17)___ and
In ___(18)___ with ___(19)___

Here's what the numbered spaces mean:
1 = your business name

Profile Your Target Market   67

2 = short description of exactly who you want to sell to

3 = a listing of their industry or niche, and their physical location

4, 5 & 6 = the things they like to do in their down time

7 = what they're thinking about that you can help them with

8, 10 & 12 = problems they're having or "itches to scratch"

9, 11 & 13 = education, advice or solutions you can offer to their problems

14, 16 & 18 = media they consume (read, watch, listen to, etc.)

15, 17 & 19 = some content that you produce that directly or indirectly promotes what you have to sell

Notice that the plan starts out with a statement about who your target market is. Yes, it's a simplified version, but again this is just a basic plan. It goes on to talk about their interests, and where you'll place your messages so that they're sure to see them.

The target market of Joe's Garage is married men with children. They work in white collar jobs in the Onondaga County area. For entertainment, they enjoy televised sports, fantasy sport leagues, and a quick beer away from their family. The conversation in their head we want to enter is about keeping their auto running so they can get to work and spend money on their family. We can help them with the following things:

- *Keep their car running inexpensively by performing regular maintenance on it*
- *Get them back on the road quickly by stocking the parts to fix drive trains quickly*

- *Removing minor dents and fixing scrapes by keeping dent pullers and different paints on hand*

They can trip over us in the following ways:

- *In local bars with the drink coasters we supply*
- *On the Internet with the local fantasy leagues we sponsor and*
- *On our blog with our advice on minor maintenance they can do at home*

* * * * *

The target market of Knitting Corner LLC is local stay-at-home moms and retired women. They live in the affluent housing developments in the suburbs of Gatlinburg. For entertainment, they enjoy knitting, sewing, and other crafts. The conversation in their head we want to enter is about how they can enjoy a hobby where the results benefit others. We can help them with the following things:

- *Getting quality supplies by asking them what they want and keeping it in stock*
- *Finding specialty products by working with small suppliers to find specialty products*
- *Learning advanced knitting techniques by scheduling classes led by superior teachers*

They can trip over us in the following ways:

- *In complementary crafting shops with signs and recommendations*

- *On Instagram and Pinterest with pictures of our customers' projects and*
- *On local AM talk radio with our weekly crafting discussion show*

Following these steps to profile your target market and create an avatar will enable you to write a basic but effective marketing plan, pointed with laser focus at members of your target market. The final version will be short enough that you can print out one or more copies and keep the whole thing in front of you at all times.

Shared Stories

Well, we're just about done with this book on crafting and using your target market avatar profile. I thought you might be interested in hearing some stories about people who have used this process to great effect. No, they're not all my direct customers. But if they can profit from writing and using these profiles, so can you!

Martial Arts School

East City Martial Arts draws their students mainly from a 6 mile radius from their school. The neighborhood is changing, with many families now being immigrants from Eastern European countries. Their market is mostly children, brought in by their parents (and increasingly, grandparents) to help them develop discipline, honesty, and other positive qualities.

The Abramovic family has three children under age 12; two boys ages 11 and 9 and a little girl aged 6. The family immigrated to East City a year ago. Father is college educated and works an entry level white collar job in Main City, but also runs a car repair shop with other Serbian men at night and on weekends. Mother has some college education, and works part time at a retail store in Main City.

They want their children to grow up with traditional values of their home country, so they keep the family involved with a social club. But they also want the children to assimilate into US society and have American friends their own age.

Mother and Father know their children might be bullied for being "foreign" and want them to be able to protect themselves. During one of their visits to the family doctor, they saw a poster for East City Martial Arts. The parents are willing to spend a lot of their income on keeping their children healthy and protected.

Because they want their children to do well in school, and life in general, they asked their neighbors for suggestions. Many people told them that children who had a background in martial arts developed good study habits, entered prestigious schools, and went on to become adults with good jobs who continued to help support their families. East City Martial Arts has been in business for over 40 years, so some immigrant families have older children and young adults who attended the school, and have been happy with the results.

Mother and Father do not like using credit to pay for things, so they either make monthly payments, or save up until they can pay for something in one lump sum. With three children at the school, they drop off a check every month. If the check is not early each month, it is delivered on the date due - they have never been late with a payment.

The Abramovic family is friends with other families with young children who have immigrated to the US, and will recommend East City Martial Arts to them. They also have some extended family in the area as well, and will recommend the school to those family members as well.

Massage Therapist

George opened his own business when he became a Licensed Massage Therapist. He struggled for a few months until he lucked into being asked to provide an afternoon of massages at a scrapbooking retreat. Many of those women made appointments with him at his business, and referred their friends. His business exploded almost overnight. He sat down one weekend and examined his client list, and built the following profile.

Name: Linda - female

Age: 48

Family: Married, with 2 children (late teens, early adult)

Money: Husband works, has a good income. Linda works part-time, and has spent nearly 20 years raising her children. She's put in a lot of time, effort and money into taking care of her kids, and now feels that it's time to take care of herself as well. She has a part-time job. She puts a little of that money away, but spends the rest on herself.

Hobbies: Linda has a hobby (quilting, stamping, scrapbooking, etc.) that gets her out of the house and allows her to spend time with other mothers. These mothers go on mini-retreats for their hobby, and like to treat themselves to small indulgences while they're away. Some of these indulgences include: wine, ice cream, extra hobby equipment purchases, and massages.

Appointments: Linda had an intro therapeutic massage at scrapbooking retreat earlier this year. She and a few of her friends enjoyed their time on my table. I offered them a follow-up appointment at my office 20 miles away for a discounted price. Most of the women who had the initial massage booked a discounted appointment.

Linda and 2 of her other friends enjoyed their massage in my office, and began to book follow-up appointments. Her friend Becky isn't as well off, and has scheduled two additional massages about 8 weeks apart. Linda drives up to my office about once every three weeks, while her friend Marcy - a health care professional herself - has been visiting every week on her day off.

New Patients: The two best ways to reach new patients like Linda and her friends are 1) to continue to do "massage parties" at hobby weekends, and 2) to ask satisfied customers to refer us to their friends. Because I perform therapeutic massage as opposed to "rubdowns," women with minor physical ailments feel relief, and understand the benefits of repeated visits. I've been updating my website every couple of weeks, letting existing customers know how I'm growing and improving the therapy space. They seem to be happy with that. I'm also investigating placing ads on web sites of the groups I've already visited, and perhaps some others.

Hair Stylist

After working in other styling salons for years, Freida decided to open her own salon near her house. While she had developed her own clients over the years, many were growing older, or simply didn't want to drive across town to her new location. She realized she would have to find a new group of clients to keep her doors open, and so she could add at least one other stylist to the salon.

I will be targeting two groups of clients for my new salon. We live near a very affluent area, where there are several assisted living and nursing home facilities. I am contacting the directors of these facilities and offering to come in once or twice a week to give basic service - trims and styling, manicure and pedicure service. We can either bill the nursing home for these services, or the residents can pay individually. Additionally, we'll set up visits to our salon for residents interested in more involved services like washes and coloring or perms.

When we develop one set of clients, I will use happy residents in posters and mailings that I will send to the other facilities to try to drum up business.

At the new salon, I will specialize in complicated hair-do's for weddings and during prom season. I am looking for another stylist who can complement my skills, doing other work.

We will also go after women moving into the area. Women who already have a stylist are very unlikely to switch unless the stylist moves or the salon closes. There is a salon nearby that I have heard might close, and I plan on contacting the owner to see about getting her to refer her customers to my salon, or maybe even buying her list outright.

Web Hosting

Juan was looking for a business he could run part-time, that also paid fairly well. He decided that hosting web sites was the way to go. A few minutes of research showed that most other hosting companies were going after the small consumers with lowball pricing. Realizing that small companies wanted quality hosting and had the money to pay for it, but not the time to manage it, Juan built the following profile.

Greta

Greta Beemish went to school for art. She was a pretty good designer in college, even sold a small number of paintings. But trying to sell paintings through brokers and galleries wasn't bringing in a consistent income, so "real jobs" that paid the bills replaced artwork. Her twenties got away from her.

Greta gets most of her news from a local news blog and other web sites. She says she doesn't subscribe to print magazines, but she often stops in at her local book store for a coffee, and winds up reading many of the art magazines there.

She was talking to her best friend on the eve of her thirtieth birthday when panic set in. She had dreamed of being a successful artist, but she wasn't even trying any more. So for her birthday, she set up a web site, ordered some business cards, rented an office and launched a business selling art prints.

When a month passed and she hadn't sold a thing, she tapped her credit card and spent several thousand dollars on advertisements. Another month, and no response.

Someone told Greta her business "ought to be on Facebook." She watched a couple videos on YouTube and put up a page. Somehow - she wasn't sure exactly how - the page brought in a message inquiring about "art for business." After a short email exchange, where she confessed to her prospect she wasn't sure about "art for business," the prospect disappeared.

At a Chamber of Commerce meeting she attended, one of the other members told her she needed a newsletter. Greta wrote and posted three monthly newsletters, but couldn't tell if anyone had even read them. In the meantime, a broker sent her a check for a piece that had sold months before. Greta didn't even know who bought the painting.

* * * * *

I'm looking for small business owners and entrepreneurs who have the time and energy to run their own business, but not to run their own web sites. They want to concentrate on their core business, not the business of hosting their site and making sure it stays up. They have enough income to pay a quality hosting service. We'll handle their web site, and they can worry about their other marketing efforts.

Used Car Dealership

Auto Works - literally a Mom and Pop business - has been selling used cars for over 30 years. Their sales have fallen off drastically in the past ten years because they haven't updated their marketing efforts. Daughter Judy has stepped in to help run the daily operation, and after a marketing audit decided she needed to make some drastic changes. The market her parents were pursuing has gotten older, and is no longer buying cars at all. Judy surveyed her market, and developed this avatar.

Fred and Marcie are a young Caucasian couple, ages 30 and 28. They have a small child, and hold two low-paying jobs between them. They are likely to live within a couple miles of the used car dealership, and pass it on their way to and from their jobs, or dropping their child off at the babysitter's. Their last car, which they got from a relative, has not been well cared for, and is increasingly costly to repair.

Although there are a few print publications left in Syracuse, they're mostly read by an older population. Fred and Marcie get their news on their phones, and interact socially that way as well. They have begun to realize with the birth of their child that they need a newer vehicle, and that they need to give it regular maintenance. Their job history won't allow them to take out a loan on a new car.

Auto Works offers a low initial payment, and will take payments here at the dealership. Many other used car dealers in town offer the same thing. We capture the interest of Fred and Marcie by being local, and by offering regular maintenance and preventative care at low cost. We will begin to send out regular messages to customers who have bought cars, and those who have inquired about cars, educating readers on basic car upkeep, and why this upkeep is helpful and important.

Fred and Marcie, and most of their social group, spend a lot of time on Facebook, Instagram and other social media sites, and get their local news from TV news sites based in Syracuse. We have shifted most of the Auto Works marketing budget from print (local newspaper and periodicals) and cable TV to targeted social media. We will be testing Google ads very soon, as our target market will often look for cars that way. To capture the notice of prospects passing by, we're investing in a few large banners we'll rotate over the lot.

While Fred and Marcie are looking for a low-cost car for their growing family, other people coming to us are looking for newer used cars with low mileage. Some of those people can secure a bank loan, but at least half still choose to finance with Auto Works, and to pay here. They also appreciate our focus on preventative maintenance.

Part of our new marketing efforts will be to shoot video of satisfied customers giving testimonials, and then build advertisements around them, targeting people like the ones appearing in the video clips.

Mystery Book Author

Andrew is literally old school - he taught in universities for over 35 years. During that time, he wrote dozens of articles for scholarly journals, and three books that were used as textbooks in college level courses. He retired and took a few years off, traveling and enjoying life. During that time, he had an idea for a mystery series. But fiction sales are different than textbook sales, and the publishing world had experienced a cataclysmic shift since he'd been involved. One one hand, he couldn't hope to draw a crowd to a reading at a bookstore.

But on the other hand, he could now sell directly to interested readers and develop a loyal audience of his own.

I have two different groups I'm trying to sell to. The first collects print book series, and the second buys ebook mystery series. Print book collectors still like to spend time in book stores, browsing and attending readings. Ebook readers read online reviews, and watch virtual readings. They may still spend a lot of time in book stores, but predominantly purchase ebooks.

Pete is in his mid-sixties, and spends several hours a week in his local B&N. He likes action/adventure books, and has read numerous series in different genres. He doesn't mind one-off books, but prefers series. Pete doesn't mind getting in on a series when the first book is published. He also doesn't mind trying an ongoing or even finished series. First, Pete will read a chapter or two over coffee in the book store. If that keeps his interest, he'll buy the first book in the series and read it at home. He's only bought a complete series a couple times, and one was at a garage sale.

Norman has had a Kindle for years. He's a voracious reader. As long as he gets a decent price break, he's happy to buy a whole series at once. More than once he's quit on a series after reading only one book or less.

Both Pete and Norman are interested in the American Southwest (where my mystery series is set). They like tough action heroes like my main character Kevin, who was a Marine at the end of the Vietnam War, but has since gone on to a career in academia. They have a secondary interest in politics, and don't mind the love interest plot arc, as long as it takes a back seat to the action and heroics.

To keep their interest (and to get their contact info so I can sell future books), I offer a rotating list of "free stuff" via my web site and email list. Sometimes it's a character sketch, other times it's a short story starring a minor character. All the freebies are material surrounding and complementing the main series. I also offer "members only" stories and vignettes for download, along with virtual readings (video of me reading my work). Both my targets are interested in some or all of these things. They hang out in discussion groups - virtual or face-to-face - and I hope to have them recommend me to their friends.

Because of the focus of my novels, side groups that might be interested are: war vets, people interested in southwest US deserts, people interested in Native Americans, and people interested in politics. I expect about 90% of these people to be white males.

Acknowledgements

Where do I begin? There are so many individuals who helped to make this book a reality in one way or another.

Teaching others is the best way to learn for yourself. My clients, looking for better ways to connect with the right people to become their own clients, have helped me immensely. Finding the right words and the right examples to explain what I was trying to say has simplified the text I put into the book.

I spent many long hours sitting at the cafe in my local Barnes & Noble, carefully crafting my thoughts and then deleting whole chapters. My profound thanks to Tammy "Cash" Casciano and her staff at B&N on Route 31 in Clay, NY for the WiFi, a comfortable place to write, several white chocolate iced mochas, and aisles upon aisles of books where I could wander, muttering to myself.

I thunked and thunked, then I writered it all down, but you wouldn't be able to read it without the assistance of my life-long friend Sharon Linne. I owe her many things, including sincere gratitude and several hundred more dollars than I actually paid her to edit my writing. In addition to correcting my spelling and grammar, she called me on several instances of laziness, and asked questions that I hadn't even considered. I can only aspire to have the care and compassion she shows on a daily basis.

I simply wouldn't be here without my wife Arlene. She makes my entire life possible, and worth living. She helps others with their lives every day, and still comes home to be with me. I do not have the words to say how much I love her, even after almost thirty years.

And finally, I thank you - my readers. Without you, this book just wouldn't matter.

Thanks for reading my book! I really appreciate you grabbing a copy of *Profile Your Target Market*.

I'd like to offer you a **FREE** Target Market Action Sheet. This multi-page document will help you build your first avatar, and help you plug that description into an easy-to-use marketing plan. Valued at $9.99, it's yours totally free at this link:

pytm.ScottGardnerAuthor.com

The following offer isn't for everyone. It's for people who realize that change is necessary in order to move forward. When you're ready, contact me for an executive level marketing review. You'll get:
- ½ hour phone/Skype interview
- ½ hour feedback
- Detailed print & digital report of your current marketing status, plus recommendations for saving money, expanding your reach, and making more profit.

Normal pricing for this is $500, but through this offer alone, your price is just **$97**. Contact me at:

review@agilemarketingservices.com

If you've got questions or comments, I'd love to hear from you directly! Please visit -

www.ScottGardnerAuthor.com

Again, my sincere thanks. Have a great day!